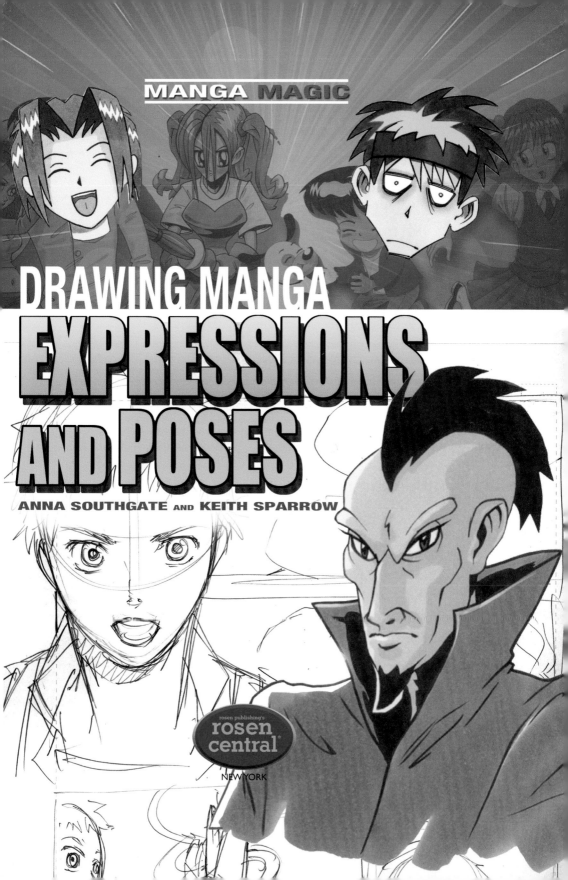

MANGA MAGIC

DRAWING MANGA
EXPRESSIONS
AND POSES

ANNA SOUTHGATE AND KEITH SPARROW

rosen publishing's
rosen
central®

NEW YORK

This edition published in 2012 by:

The Rosen Publishing Group, Inc.
29 East 21st Street
New York, NY 10010

Additional end matter copyright © 2012 by The Rosen Publishing Group, Inc.

Library of Congress Cataloging-in-Publication Data

Southgate, Anna.
Drawing manga expressions and poses / Anna Southgate, Keith Sparrow.
     p. cm.—(Manga magic)
Includes bibliographical references and index.
ISBN 978-1-4488-4800-3 (library binding: alk. paper)
ISBN 978-1-4488-4804-1 (pbk.: alk. paper)
ISBN 978-1-4488-4808-9 (6-pack: alk. paper)
1. Face in art—Juvenile literature. 2. Expression in art—Juvenile literature.
3. Human figure in art—Juvenile literature. 4. Comic books, strips, etc.—Japan—
Technique—Juvenile literature. 5. Cartooning—Technique—Juvenile literature.
I. Sparrow, Keith. II. Title.
NC1764.8.F33S68 2012
741.5'1—dc22

2011012230

4622

Manufactured in the United States of America

CPSIA Compliance Information: Batch #SI1YA: For further information, contact Rosen Publishing, New York, New York, at 1-800-237-9932.

CONTENTS

INTRODUCTION

A sweaty brow. A nervous smile. A wink of the eye. These are all ways to use facial expressions to convey emotion in a story. In manga, a great deal of information about the action shines through in the expressions and poses of the characters. Manga (mahn-gah) is a style of art that appears in Japanese comic books and graphic novels. The style is unique: characters typically have large, pronounced eyes and slender, angular bodies.

Drawing manga is fun because it allows you to create any kind of character you want. There really isn't any genre or style of story that manga hasn't affected. What can be tricky about drawing manga, though, are the facial details. But if you follow the step-by-step directions in this book, you can ensure your characters' eyes flash "determined" and not "depressed." Eyes are crucial. For instance, a sassy girl might have longer eyelashes when she's trying to win the attention of the school heartthrob. But when he turns her down, you could draw dark rings around her eyes to show her unhappiness. It's important to remember that every character you create can be truly unique when you add emotive flourishes.

A pose can also say a lot about the character you draw. Suppose you have created a cool mech warrior deep-space pilot: Does he stand up straight and take charge of every situation, or does he slouch with his hands in his flight suit pockets, waiting for the action to come to him? Conveying movement in a static image can be hard, but with practice you'll be able to make sure your character looks like he's springing into action and not crouching scared. So grab your gear and get drawing!

You do not need to spend a fortune to get started in drawing and coloring good manga art. You do, however, need to choose your materials with some care to get the best results from your work. Start with a few basics and add to your kit as your style develops and you figure out what you like working with.

Artists have their preferences when it comes to equipment. Regardless of personal favorites, you will need a basic set of materials that will enable you to sketch, ink, and color your manga art. The items discussed here are only a guide—don't be afraid to experiment to find out what works best for you.

PAPER

You will need two types of paper—one for creating sketches, the other for producing finished color artwork.

For quickly jotting down ideas, almost any piece of scrap paper will do. For more developed sketching, though, use tracing paper. Tracing paper provides a smooth surface, helping you sketch freely. It is also forgiving—any mistakes can easily be erased several times over. Typically, tracing paper comes in pads. Choose a pad that is around 24 pounds (90 grams per square meter) in weight for the best results—lighter tracing paper may buckle and heavier paper is not suitable for sketching.

Once you have finished sketching out ideas, you will need to transfer them to the paper you want to produce your finished colored art on. To do this, you will have to trace over your pencil sketch, so the paper you choose cannot be too opaque or "heavy"—otherwise you will not be able to see the sketch underneath. Choose a paper around 16 lb (60 gsm) for this.

Graphite pencils are ideal for getting your ideas down on paper and producing your initial drawing. The pencil drawing is probably the most important stage in creating your artwork. Choose an HB and a 2B to start with.

The type of paper you use is also important. If you are going to color using marker pens, use marker or layout paper. Both of these types are very good at holding the ink found in markers. Other paper of the same weight can cause the marker ink to bleed, that is, the ink soaks beyond the inked lines of your drawing and produces fuzzy edges. This does not look good.

You may wish to color your art using other materials, such as colored pencils or watercolors. Drawing paper is good for graphite pencil and inked-only art (such as

Working freehand allows great freedom of expression and is ideal when you are working out a sketch, but you will find times when precision is necessary.

Use compasses or a circle guide for circles and ellipses to keep your work sharp. Choose compasses that can be adjusted to hold both pencils and pens.

that found in the majority of manga comic books), while heavyweight watercolor paper holds wet paint and colored inks and comes in a variety of surface textures.

Again, don't be afraid to experiment: you can buy many types of paper in single sheets while you find the ones that suit your artwork best.

PENCILS

The next step is to choose some pencils for your sketches. Pencil sketching is probably the most important stage. It always comes first when producing manga art (you cannot skip ahead to the inking stage). Make sure you choose pencils that feel good in your hand and allow you to express your ideas freely.

Pencils are manufactured in a range of hard and soft leads. Hard leads are designated by the letter H and soft leads by the letter B. Both come in six levels—6H is the hardest lead and 6B is the softest. In the middle is HB, a halfway mark between the two ranges. Generally, an HB and a 2B lead will serve most sketching purposes, with the softer lead being especially useful for loose, "idea" sketches, and the harder lead for more final lines.

Alternatively, you can opt for mechanical pencils. Also called self-propelling pencils, these come in a variety of lead grades and widths. They never lose their points, making sharpening traditional wood-cased pencils a thing of the past. Whether you use one is entirely up to you—it is possible to get excellent results whichever model you choose.

SHARPENERS AND ERASERS

If you use wooden pencils, you will need to get a quality sharpener; this is a small but essential piece of equipment. Electric sharpeners work very well and are also

Felt-tip pens are the ideal way to ink your sketches. A fineliner, medium-tip pen and sign pen should meet all of your needs, whatever your style and pre-ferred subjects. A few colored felt-tip pens can be a good addi-tion to your kit, allowing you to introduce color at the inking stage.

very fast; they last a long time, too. Otherwise, a handheld sharpener is fine. One that comes with a couple of spare blades can be a worthwhile investment, ensuring that your pencils are always sharp.

Along with a sharpener, you will need an eraser for removing any visible pencil lines from your inked sketches prior to coloring. Choose a high-quality eraser that does not smudge the pencil lead, scuff the paper, or leave dirty fragments all over your work. A soft "putty" eraser works best, since it absorbs pencil lead rather than just rubbing it away. For this reason, putty erasers do become dirty with use. Keep yours clean by trimming it carefully with scissors every now and then.

INKING PENS

The range of inking pens can be bewildering, but some basic rules will help you select the pens you need. Inked lines in most types of manga tend to be quite bold, so buy a thin-nibbed pen, about 0.5 mm (.02 inches) and a medium-size nib, about 0.8 mm (.03 in). Make sure that the ink in the pens is

waterproof; this ink won't smudge or run. Next, you will need a medium-tip felt pen. Although you won't need to use this pen very often to ink the outlines of your characters, it is still useful for filling in small detailed areas of solid black. The Pentel sign pen does this job well. Last, consider a pen that can create different line widths according to the amount of pressure you put on the tip. These pens replicate brushes and allow you to create flowing lines such as those seen on hair and clothing. The Pentel brush pen does this very well, delivering a steady supply of ink to the tip from a replaceable cartridge.

Test-drive a few pens at your art store to see which ones suit you best. All pens should produce clean, sharp lines with a deep black pigment.

MARKERS AND COLORING AIDS

Many artists use markers, rather than paint, to color their artwork because markers are easy to use and come in a huge variety of colors and shades. Good-quality markers, such as those made by Chartpak, Letraset, or Copic, produce excellent, vibrant results. They allow you to build up multiple layers of color so that you can create rich, detailed work and precise areas of shading.

Markers come in a wide variety of colors, which allows you to achieve subtle variations in tone. In addition to a thick nib for broad areas of color, the Copic markers shown here feature a thin nib for fine detail.

Make sure that you use your markers with marker or layout paper to avoid bleeding. Markers are often refillable, so they last a long time. The downside is that they are expensive, so choose a limited number of colors to start with, and add as your needs evolve. As always, test out a few markers in the art store before buying any.

Markers are not the only coloring media. Paints and gouache also produce excellent results, and can give your work a distinctive look. Add white gouache, which comes in a tube, to your work to create highlights and sparkles of light. Apply it in small quantities with a good-quality watercolor brush.

It is also possible to color your artwork on a computer. This is quick to do, although obviously there is a high initial cost. It also tends to produce flatter color than markers or paints.

DRAWING AIDS

Most of your sketching will be done freehand, but there are situations, especially with human-made objects such as the edges of buildings or the wheels of a car, when your line work needs to be crisp and sharp to create the right look. Rulers, circle guides, and compasses all provide this accuracy. Rulers are either metal or plastic; in most cases, plastic ones work best, though metal ones tend to last longer. For circles, use a circle guide, which is a plastic sheet with a wide variety of different-sized holes stamped out of it. If the circle you want to draw is too big for the circle guide, use a compass that can hold a pencil and inking pen.

A selection of warm and cool grays is a useful addition to your marker colors. Most ranges feature several different shades. These are ideal for shading on faces, hair, and clothes.

VIEW FROM ABOVE

Drawing views from above involves foreshortening, which is a way of showing how the eye interprets distances in unusual perspectives. Here, the torso will be dramatically shorter than usual, and the feet will be smaller to indicate the distance from the eye. The character is looking up at the viewer so that the face will be clearly visible. This makes the pose more dramatic.

Draw an egg shape with the chin facing off to one side. Use an ellipse and triangle for the pelvis, lines for the legs and arms, and a circle for the shoulder joint.

Start to flesh out the body by adding a torso. Then draw in the arms, with elbows and hands. Complete this stage by drawing the legs, with knee joints, and feet.

Note that there is no neck visible from this angle. Now add facial features: large manga eyes, eyebrows, a tiny nose, and a mouth. Add hair and fingers.

Start to add clothing details: the collar and sleeves of the shirt, the ribbing on the sweater vest and socks, and the skirt. Add her shoes last.

This time go to the next stage and ink your drawing. Choose the most important lines to ink, and work carefully on top of the pencil marks. You can use solid black in some areas to give your drawing more impact, such as the shadow under the chin, and her shoes. Add some fine lines to indicate creases and folds in the clothing.

KNEELING, LEANING FORWARD

Drawing a figure with bended arms or legs can present a new challenge. This character is kneeling down and leaning toward the viewer. Her weight is supported by her outstretched arms and she is looking attentively with a slightly tilted head.

Draw an egg head, a curving line for the back and ovals for the buttocks and thighs. Draw a curving horizontal out to the shoulders, and lines for the arms.

Add the neck and shoulders, then give her a torso. Next give her arms, with hands on the floor, then flesh out her legs, and add a foot.

Put in the facial features of large eyes with eyebrows, tiny nose, and mouth. Add long flowing hair, then start to block out the darkest areas of the drawing.

Ink all the main lines of the drawing. Then ink the area of neck where the collar sits, and the swimsuit. Leave some areas white to add color detail later.

When the ink is dry, erase the pencil lines. Color her skin pale pink, then give her some red hair, leaving a white highlight on each side. Finally use a mid blue for the areas of detail on the swimsuit.

STANDING WITH ATTITUDE

As a graphic storytelling medium, manga relies heavily on body language to convey the personality and moods of its characters. This manga girl is standing with her arms folded and her weight on her back leg, with an arched back and slightly inclined head, giving her a sulky, confrontational look.

Draw an egg-shaped head, then a center line. Bisect this and add circles for shoulder joints and lines for arms. Add a triangle for the pelvis and stick legs and feet.

Flesh out the arms and add a torso by joining the arms and pelvis. Draw circles for the hip joints, then draw in the legs. Add in large ellipses for the feet.

She is looking away to her left, so give her pupils that are looking in this direction. Add eyebrows, nose, and mouth, then give her some shaggy cropped hair.

Now work on the details of the clothing. She is wearing a fitted cropped top with a collar, tight jeans with a belt, and large futuristic boots.

Ink the main lines, then use solid black for the shadow on the neck. Ink in the cuff of a glove, then use a fineliner to indicate folds in the clothing.

SITTING PRETTY

A sitting posture is an interesting challenge to a manga artist. Here is a girl in a long demure dress, sitting attentively on a large footstool. Her hands are clasped between her knees and her back is arched up, giving her an innocent air.

Draw an egg head and a curving center line, then bisect the line with a horizontal line. Add circles for the shoulder joints and lines for the arms. Draw an ellipse for the pelvis and circles for the knees.

Join the head and shoulders, and flesh out the arms. Give her a torso. Add flesh to the top of her left leg by joining the hip and knee joints. Add both lower legs and the pointed feet.

Now start to get some detail into her face and clothing. Add large eyes, a tiny nose, and a smiling mouth. Give her shoulder-length straight hair and spiky bangs. She is wearing a fitted demure dress and ballet pumps.

Ink all the main lines of her face, figure, and clothing, then ink around the footstool, and block out the shadow areas on her legs and on the stool legs. Color her hair, leaving white highlights on the crown and on each side of her head.

Use the signpen to color the pumps. Then color her face, neck, the bit of visible hand, and her legs pale pink. Use darker pink to create the shadow cast by her hair on her face and neck. Finally use a bright red to color her dress.

RUNNING FAST

In this pose the straight leading leg is showing the speed of the girl's movement, and there is a slight foreshortening on the trailing leg. Note in a running stance how the arms and legs operate on opposite sides, so if the left leg is forward, then the right arm is also forward, and vice versa.

Draw a balloon-shaped head with pointed chin. Add a center line. Use circles for the shoulders, elbow, hips, and knees, and join with lines for the legs and arms. Add simple fists.

Flesh out the body. Add a neck, work along the arms and fists, then down the torso. Work down the nearest leg, adding a running shoe, then flesh out the back leg and shoe.

Give her eyes, a nose, a mouth, and one ear. Add spiky bangs and tied-back hair. Create the T-shirt and shorts, add socks, and refine the shoes.

Work around the figure, inking the main lines of the head, body, clothing, and shoes. Use the inking pen to add folds in the clothing and socks. When the ink is dry, erase any pencil lines.

Color her skin pale pink, and blend in red-brown shadows. Give her bright blue hair, with darker blue shadows. Add blue-gray for the T-shirt. Finally, color the shoes pink.

RUNNING LEAP

Here, a tough-looking action girl in a futuristic jumpsuit leaps into view. Her long flowing hair trails behind her, giving a useful emphasis to her movement. Her left leg is bent tightly forward at the knee, suggesting she has just used this leg to push off from a point behind. The body is tightly compacted for flight, except for the right leg, which is stretched out ready for a landing.

Create an egg-shaped head with pointed chin, then use a curved line for the spine. Use circles for the shoulder joints, elbow, and knees, and a large circle for the hip. Add straight lines for the bent arm and both the legs.

Add some detail to the body. Add the neck and flesh out the torso. Add the arms and legs, making the top of the leg closest to you fairly muscular. Draw in simply shaped hands and feet.

Next work on the facial details, giving her large expressive eyes with arched eyebrows, and a small nose and mouth. Use a few simple lines to create her hair, which is streaming out behind her.

Start to add some detail to her clothing, then use your pencil to create areas of shading on her top and cuffs, and on the flashes on her pants. Give her pumping fists and shade these, too.

Ink all the main lines of your composition. Then use the fineliner to indicate some folds in the clothing around the elbow and knees. When the ink is dry, carefully erase any pencil lines you no longer need.

15

OVER THE SHOULDER

A good understanding of the figure from all sides will be useful when tackling an unusual pose like this. A beautiful but tough-looking girl looks back over her shoulder toward you. Her weight is balanced evenly and her knees are slightly bent in case a fast movement is necessary. The forward tilt of the head indicates a guarded curiosity, as if she's heard a noise behind her that might be a threat. Her outfit is feminine but practical, loose around the legs but with tight cuffs.

Draw an egg-shaped head with a pointed chin, and a curved spine. Add circles for the shoulders and elbows, and join with lines. Draw two ellipses for the buttocks and a straight line for the waist, and join these to create hips. Draw lines for the legs and triangles for the feet.

Join the head and shoulder line to create a neck. Draw the curve of her visible side, then flesh out the arms and legs. Note that only one hand can be seen.

With the basic body in place, it's time to add facial details. Give her large eyes, a button nose, and a tiny mouth. Add the ear that can be seen, then give her spiky bangs and use a few pencil lines to indicate hair.

Add clothing details. She has a stand-up collar and sash trim over her right shoulder. Loose and flowing below-the-knee pants complete her outfit.

MODEL BEHAVIOR

This character is striking a tongue-in-cheek modelling pose, as suggested by one hand on the hip and the other playing with her hair. She's coyly bending her left leg, and she has a happy smiling expression with closed eyes. Note the small, pointed ears, which are a feature on many manga characters, and give a slight fantasy air. Long blazing orange hair completes the look.

Start with an egg shape for the head. Add a center line and a shoulder line. Add circles for the shoulder, hip, knee, and elbow joints, and lines for the limbs.

Flesh out the body, working from the neck along the arms and down the torso and legs. Draw the fingers of her right hand on her hip.

Get some detailing into her face. Her eyes are narrow slits, and her mouth is a grin. Add spiky bangs and knee-length flowing locks down her back.

Add details on the clothes. She is wearing a cropped top and shorts with white trimming. Shade these lightly in pencil. Add shoes, and a couple of bangles on her wrist.

Ink, then color your girl. Use pale pink for her skin, leaving white highlights and adding dark beige shadows. Give her striking orange hair, leaving a white highlight on top. To complement the orange, make her suit and pumps acid green.

WALKING ON AIR

Here is a simple but graceful pose, which can be used to indicate a happy carefree mood or a free-spirited girl. Her expression is wide-eyed and smiling, and she has one leg bent up at the knee and her arms stretched out wide on both sides of her, as if she's enjoying the breeze blowing over her. In manga a character can literally defy gravity and walk on air if the mood strikes her.

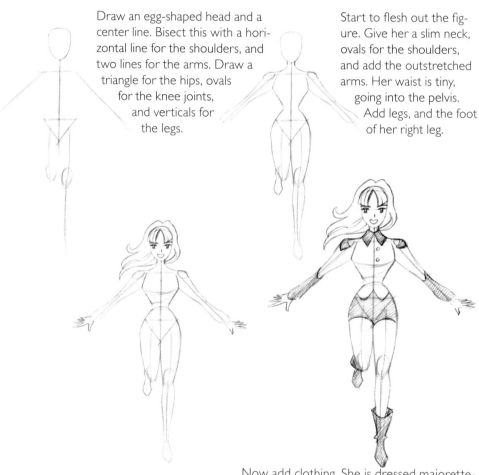

Draw an egg-shaped head and a center line. Bisect this with a horizontal line for the shoulders, and two lines for the arms. Draw a triangle for the hips, ovals for the knee joints, and verticals for the legs.

Start to flesh out the figure. Give her a slim neck, ovals for the shoulders, and add the outstretched arms. Her waist is tiny, going into the pelvis. Add legs, and the foot of her right leg.

Add facial features: large eyes, a small nose, and an open mouth. Give her spiky bangs and flowing hair. Add her hands and outstretched fingers.

Now add clothing. She is dressed majorette-style in a buttoned shirt with collar and epaulettes, shorts, and boots. Shade the collar, epaulettes, shorts, and boots; only the cuff and foot of the right boot can be seen.

SITTING DAYDREAMING

Nothing beats a quiet moment sitting and daydreaming. Imagine this manga girl sitting on the grass on a cool summer evening. Her hands are clasping her shins and she's looking happily upward at the viewer, with her head tilted backward in an open and relaxed pose.

Draw an oval head, two circles for the two shoulder joints and the hip, a rectangle with a curved profile for the torso, and straight lines for the arms and legs.

Create the basic profile. Her back is a curve: sketch one line joining both shoulder joints, and one from the chin down. Add the legs.

Make two parallel horizontal lines across her face and use these as guides for her large eyes and tiny ears. Add a nose and mouth, then flesh out the arms.

Start to ink your sketch, concentrating on the most important lines. Add more facial detail, inking the pupils and around the twin highlights in each eye. Outline the mouth and add two or three tiny vertical lines to the nose.

Add spiky bangs, with a ponytail down her back. Then start to indicate her clothing: she is wearing a cropped top with detailing around the neck and down the front, and shorts with cuff detail. Indicate the top of her boots.

WIELDING A SWORD

Not all manga girls are shy and fragile creatures. Here is a good example of a confident action girl who is ready for a fight with sword poised. Her stance is balanced with legs apart for stability, and the long sash at her waist is used to give a dramatic effect of movement and tension.

Draw an oval head, and a center line down to a triangle for the pelvis. Add lines for the legs, with ovals for the knee joints. Add oval shoulder and elbow joints.

Add flesh to your basic shape. Join the neck and shoulders, then create a torso, with trim waist. Add legs and feet, then the arms.

Work in facial features of eyes, nose, and mouth. Add a spiky hairdo: continue this down to her waist. Draw a sword in her hands, and start to indicate clothing.

Ink in the main lines of your sketch. Then use a brush pen to color in the black areas of her costume: the fitted top, and the detail on the pants and shoes. There is an area of shadow on the skirt cape, and a fold in its band.

The outfit has a bold black-and-white pattern, so minimal color can be used. Add some light gray shadows to the arms and legs to give depth, then color her face and neck a fleshy pink, with darker beige shadows under the fringe and neck. Use an orange for the pupils, and add some pale mauve shadow to her white hair. Add gold color to the sword hilt, and a rich purple to the sash. Finish with some soft white pencil highlights on the sash and body, and some blue-gray shadows on the blade.

DOWN ON ONE KNEE

A difficult pose to get right is kneeling down, which again requires a good knowledge of your character's body shape. Here is a warrior girl taking a moment of rest. She is propping herself up with her traditional katana sword in its sheath, and surveying the view. Her body is balanced with left knee up and the right on the ground, with her right hand resting across the thigh.

Draw circles for the head, shoulder joints, and one visible elbow, with lines to join the shoulders and for the arms. Draw a curved spine, and an oval for the hip joint. The legs at this stage are both angled lines.

Refine the profile of her face, then add a neck. Add a torso with a trim waist, and two curves for breasts. Flesh out her left arm, adding an outline hand. Next flesh out her legs. Both are bent at the knee: the knee of her right leg is on the ground, while her left knee is in the air, with her foot steadying her. Indicate both feet.

Work next on her facial features. Give her large eyes with double highlights, eyebrows, a snub nose, and small mouth. Add her right ear and flesh out her right arm, adding fingers resting on her left thigh. Now indicate the sword: this runs behind her hand and down to the ground on a plane with her right leg and left toe. Draw a line for the hilt.

Give her a hairband, and then add spiky hair above it and down her back. Now start to get some details into the clothing. Give her a military-style jacket with stand-up collar, fabric closures, and decorative flashes on the sleeves. Her pants also have decorative flashes. Then add detail to the sword.

The coloring is a dull, military-style gray for the uniform, with bright yellow trim. Use a pale beige for the skin, and a bright green for her hair. Use darker tones for shading to give extra weight to the figure.

Ink in the main lines of your sketch. Refine the clothing details and add detail to the boots. Create a rectangular pattern on the sword. Next use black to color her pupils, and create the shadow on her neck and on the underside of the hilt.

POPULAR FEMALE POSES

There are several poses that recur in manga time and time again, and it is worth drawing these so that you can tell more of your story through your characters' body language, as well as through their faces and clothes.

below This pose is worried: the girl is anxious and nervous. Her knees are knocked together and she is slightly hunched over in a defensive body position.

above This is a demure, submissive girl in a Japanese kimono. Breaking free of tradition and leading the exciting life of a modern young woman is a common theme.

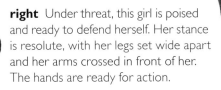

above Here's a girl who is running away from something in alarm. She is leaning forward and away from the danger, while her eyes are glancing fearfully back toward it.

right Under threat, this girl is poised and ready to defend herself. Her stance is resolute, with her legs set wide apart and her arms crossed in front of her. The hands are ready for action.

left Assertive, but not in the least aggressive, this is a confident pose. The girl is sitting in a comfortable pose, looking happy and slightly mischievous.

below With her feet planted firmly on the floor, and her hand brought up into a fist, this girl has a gutsy air. This is a common pose in manga, designed to say, "I did it."

right With fists at the ready and fiery hair, this is a feisty pose. Even though she is wearing a stylish dress, this girl is not afraid to get her hands dirty.

left This girl has a wistful pose, as if daydreaming. Her chin is resting on her hands and her knees are together with her feet apart. She's gazing into the distance with a slight smile and her eyes show a hint of concentration.

GALLERY

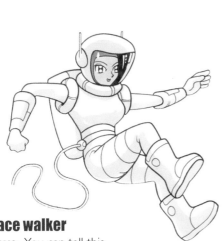

space walker
above You can tell this girl is cute, even in a space suit. The suit itself is designed to look feminine, but is still functional enough for a space walk.

leaping into action
right This girl is jumping into position with a staff at the ready. Her clothing is cute, but has the look of a military uniform about it. Her expression is determined.

superheroine
above Streaking through the air, this girl is on her way to right some wrongs. She has a typical figure-hugging leotard with a cape, and has long flowing hair to make her more feminine.

boiling hot
right Cowering from a source of great heat, this girl is flushed and there are drops of sweat falling from her face. All the colors in this sketch suggest heat.

GALLERY

boxer

right Here is a sporty character with spiky, swept-back hair and functional top and shorts. Her boxing gloves show she's in a fight and the athletic stance says she won't be a pushover.

magical girl

above This is a happy character: her smiling eyes and broad grin need a simple style to emphasize her personality.

freezing cold

below This girl is frost-bitten. Her body is thin and she's hugging herself to try and keep warm. Her knees are turned inward and the pale blue lines suggest she is shivering.

schoolgirl

left This typical schoolgirl with sailor-suit type uniform is being surprised by a cute little creature. She has a sweet innocent look that is enhanced by her stance.

RUNNING HEADLONG

With male manga characters, the body can be drawn in a slightly more forceful pose. This example is a young male tearing full-speed into an aggressive position, with fists clenched and head set forward. The leading leg is bent at the knee and is curving outward in a dynamic flowing shape. The torso is nearly horizontal, which emphasizes the onrushing posture.

Draw an egg-shaped head with pointed chin. Draw three circles for the two shoulder joints and one visible elbow joint, and join with a curved line. Add a curved line for the spine, and a triangle for the pelvis. Add ovals for knee joints and lines for the legs.

Add flesh to the torso, arms, legs, and feet. Add fists to both arms. Draw in his left ear.

Start to add facial features: large eyes and tiny nose and mouth. Give him some spiky hair. Then start to add costume details. Give him a clenched left fist.

Ink the main lines using a thick nib. Add some creases to his clothes, then use black ink to color his pupils, the shadow under his chin, and his hair.

STRIDING ALONG

This is a more relaxed pose, showing a teenager strolling along in a positive, carefree manner. Remember to have opposite limbs leading, for example: left leg, right arm forward. Both feet are in contact with the ground in this walking pose, with toes on the right leg and heel on the left down, and his arms are swinging loosely by his sides.

Add a neck and shoulders, then flesh out the arms. Draw the legs, from the hip joints down to the knee joint: his left leg is in front of his right and moving forward. Add the lower legs.

Draw an oval head. Add a vertical spine. Bisect this, and add circles for the shoulder and elbow joints with lines for the limbs. Add a triangle for the pelvis, one knee joint, and four lines for the legs.

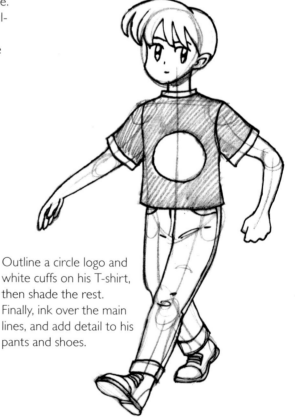

Give him facial features: eyes with double highlights, and tiny nose and mouth. Add spiky bangs and simple hair. Add hands, one open and one fist.

Outline a circle logo and white cuffs on his T-shirt, then shade the rest. Finally, ink over the main lines, and add detail to his pants and shoes.

STANDING FIRM

Here's a confident, no-nonsense pose for a young male. He's standing tall and straight, with arms folded but a slight tilt to the head, which indicates a cautious manner. The legs are slightly apart, too, which gives him a solid, stable stance, as if to imply he's not about to be moved, no matter what happens.

Draw an inverted egg for the head, and a vertical spine, with a triangle for the pelvis. Draw circles for the shoulder, elbow, and knee joints, with lines for the limbs.

Start to flesh out the body. Add a collar, shoulders, torso, and the arms, one folded over the other. Give him flared pants and simply shaped shoes.

Add facial features and outline the spiky hair. Create clothing details: the V-neck, belt, and flashes on the pants and top. Add the soles of the shoes.

Ink all the main lines, then use your black to color the hair, leaving a white flash, and create shadow on the neck and under the arms. Add detail on the knees.

Keep the coloring simple. Use pale pink for the skin of his face, neck, and hands, with a dark beige for shadows. Use a bright blue for his uniform.

RECOIL

This character is pulling back in alarm from some sudden threat or danger. The body is leaning backward, and the leading leg is turned inward in preparation for turning the whole body away. His left arm is pulled back and counter-balancing the sudden shift in weight, and his casual suit is flowing away from the body to exaggerate the movement.

Start to flesh out the body, creating shoulders and torso. Add one bent arm and one straight, and legs. Add basic shapes for the arms and feet.

Create an inverted egg shape for the head, an angled line for the spine, a triangle for the pelvis, with circles for the shoulder and knee joints. Add lines for the limbs.

Refine the profile of the face, and add facial features: eyes, mouth, and ear. Then give your character a mop of spiky hair. Add fingers to both hands.

Now work up the clothing. He has a high-collared shirt, loose jacket, and baggy pants with a belt. Add some detail to the shoes on his feet.

ATTACK AND DEFEND

As the saying goes, the best form of defense is attack, and here is an example of a typical action manga character in a battle stance, shield up and sword poised to strike. His rear leg is bent to brace his weight against attack and to enable him to push forward quickly. He has turned his body side-on to limit the attack area, and his face is set in an angry and defiant snarl.

Use an inverted egg shape for the head, with a circle for his right shoulder joint. Draw a circle for his left elbow joint with two lines for the limb. Draw a center vertical, then obscure most of it with the shape of the shield. His right leg is a single line; his left leg is a Z-shape with a circle for the knee joint.

Next work on the details of the face. Add big eyes with double highlights and arched eyebrows. His mouth is wide open and his teeth are visible. Add a headband with a mass of spiky hair.

Now start to flesh out the body. There is a little torso showing on his right-hand side. Add his muscular right arm and clenched right fist in a gauntlet. Draw his left shoulder and the fingers of his left hand, then flesh out his legs, adding heavy boots to both.

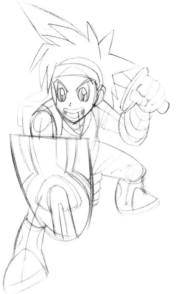

Start to add details. There are several layers of clothing at the neck, in addition to straps for his backpack, and oval motifs on both pant legs. Draw in the sword, and add decorative details to the shield.

Give your warrior pale blue eyes and acid green hair, with a brown headband. His skin is pink with a darker pink in his open mouth. Color his costume blue, working over this in shadow areas to strengthen the color. Use a dark leather color for his backpack, then work the boots, shield, and hilt in shades of brown, honey, and yellow. Finally, add ice blue to the blade and gauntlets.

Ink the main lines of your drawing and indicate some creases around the knee of his left leg. Then use black to create shadows at the sides of his mouth and on the gauntlet on his left hand.

COMING AT YOU

Here is a pose that involves a dynamic body shape with some foreshortening to emphasize the forward movement. The character is running full tilt toward the viewer and letting loose with a flying punch. Note how the forward knee is curved inward, and the trailing leg is smaller to increase the distance from the viewer. The punching arm cuts diagonally across the body.

Draw an inverted egg head with a vertical line down to a triangle for the pelvis. Draw ovals for the elbows, shoulders, and one knee joint, with lines for the limbs.

Flesh out the upper body, adding arms and fists, and the torso. Add eyes and eyebrows, with a small nose and mouth, then draw a crown of spiky hair.

Add his legs; one is drawn from the hip to the knee joint and has only a foot visible. This obscures the full-length right leg. Lightly shade his hair and shorts.

Use a thick nib to ink the main lines. Then color the shorts and hair black. Create a round neck and sleeves for his top. Finally, create a six-pack on his torso.

WIDE POWER STANCE

An altogether different stance is this squatting figure with outstretched arms and wide open hands. The figure is dynamically low to the ground and almost symmetrical in its stability. The outfit suggests a street fighter of some sort, and his stance could be a deflective one, or he could be getting set to unleash some kind of power blast from his open palms.

Bisect an inverted egg head with a curved line and add triangle hands. Add a short line to a triangle pelvis, then add legs and feet in an inverted Z-shape.

Create wide shoulders and muscled arms, then a muscular torso down to the waist. Clothe the leg lines with baggy pants that hang in loose folds.

Add facial features: here, slit eyes and an open mouth. Add ears and a simple spiky haircut, then indicate wrist and belly wraps. Add a sash and kung fu slippers.

Ink all the main lines of the sketch. Create detail on the palms, and then indicate lots of folds on the bottoms of the pant legs to get some movement here.

Color his skin pale pink with a darker shade for the open mouth. Give him yellow hair, gray-brown pants and slippers, and a bright red sash.

FLYING PUNCH

The figure in manga can often be graceful and balletic, such as this flying punch pose. It's drawn in profile to get the most out of the action. His clothes are simple and designed for combat, and he's barefoot and bare-armed for an austere, focused appearance.

Draw an oval head with a vertical line down to a circle knee joint, and add a line for the lower leg. Add an oval pelvis, a circle and two lines for the leg, and a line and six circles for his shoulder, elbow joints, and fists.

Flesh out the torso, arms, and legs, all of which are muscular. Then, give him a fierce facial profile with feline nose and open mouth. Add an eye and eyebrow, together with an ear.

Add a lion's-mane hairstyle, shaggy on top with a ponytail down his back. Then draw a clenched fist on his left arm, and fingers on his right hand.

Ink the main lines, adding costume details, including torn edges to his shirt and pant legs. Use black to create wristbands, and shadows on his hair and leg.

Color his skin using pink and beige, building shadow as necessary. Make his suit red, with a white highlight on his left thigh. Finally, color his hair in two shades of blue.

THREAT BEHIND

Another type of action pose is this figure, who's turning to face a threat from behind. His long, spidery legs and arms are typical of many manga characters. His weight is balanced evenly between both legs, and his left arm is raised defensively to counter a blow.

Start with an oval head, circles for the shoulder joints, and lines for the shoulders, arms, and spine. Add an ellipse for the hip with lines and circles for the legs.

Flesh out the head and body. The face is in profile: give him a bushy eyebrow, an eye, nose, and mouth. He has a shock of hair and a pumping fist.

Next add clothes to the body. He is wearing a T-shirt, open jacket with high collar and patch details, and tight pants. Draw in his pointed boots.

Begin inking. Go over all the main lines of his face, body, and clothing. Include the creases in his clothes. Ink his eye and eyebrow and his black hair.

Now color your figure. His face and hands are shades of pink, and his clothes are shades of brown and gray. Color the patches on his sleeves yellow.

JUMPING FOR JOY

Not all manga males are grim fighters. This boy, for example, is a gleeful youth, jumping for joy. He's wearing simple clothing of a T-shirt and jeans, and carrying a backpack, which suggests he's on his way to or from school. The head is drawn larger in relation to the body, which makes him look younger, and his arms and legs have an elastic quality, which gives a more cartoony feel.

Detail the face, which is dominated by the huge open mouth with broad lips. His eyes are simply closed slits with eyebrows. Draw his ears and give him a spiky short hairstyle.

Draw a round head, a vertical center line, a line for the shoulders with circles for the elbows, a broad ellipse for the pelvis, with circles and lines for the knee joints and legs.

Add flesh to the bones, and give the character some clothes. The shirt is loose and has short sleeves. Draw arms and legs, and simple shapes for hands.

Finish your sketch by giving him pants and shoes, and fleshing out the arms and hands. As a finishing touch, add the straps of a backpack, and shade them.

CREEPING AROUND

Here's another example of a more cute and cartoon-style figure. This character is peering nervously around a corner. His body is bent forward with his weight on the front leg and his left arm cautiously out in front. The figure is supported on the toes of his right foot, and his rear arm is tucked in behind. The eyes are wide open as he peeps around, and his manner suggests someone creeping.

Start with an oval head, with circles for the shoulder, elbow, and hand. Join these with a curved line. Add an ellipse for the hip, circle for the knee, and lines for the leg and foot.

Add details for the face. The eye is large, featuring a pupil with a highlight. The nose is small, and the mouth expresses determination. Give him lots of spiky, cropped hair, outline a highlight, and add an ear.

Now add clothes to the lines of the body. He is wearing a loose hoodie and jeans, which are baggy below the knees. Add large fingers to his hand, and a sneaker on his foot.

His right leg needs to be added now. This is bent back, and also has a jeans leg and sneaker. Finally, at this stage, indicate the corner of a wall: he is looking around this.

Ink your sketch. Outline his facial features, hand, and clothing. Also ink the corner of the wall. Then, using a thick-nibbed inking pen, and leaving the highlight white, ink his hair and an area of shadow on his tummy.

PUNCHING AT YOU

This is an unusual pose for a manga story, as it is reminiscent of the mainstream superhero characters in Western comics. It is a useful pose and worth practicing. The character is flying or leaping toward you with fist outstretched. His outfit is skintight superhero-style.

Draw an oval head and a center line, bisected by a horizontal line for the shoulders. Add circles for the shoulder joints, a triangle for the pelvis, and lines for the legs.

Add the basic shape of the arm, then position the fist: this is the focal point of the sketch. Flesh out the body, then clothe the legs and suggest feet.

Next add the facial details: large eyes with double highlights, button nose, and small mouth. Suggest a hairline. Then work up both hands, including the fist.

Ink the main lines of the figure. Then use black to create shadow under the neck, on the fist, on his right arm, and on his feet. Add his eyes, and hair, with a highlight.

Use honey and maroon to create his clothing. Leave areas of white highlight on his pants to suggest they are made of a shiny fabric. Leave white areas on his punching fist and around his collar. Color his face pale pink.

HEROIC POINTING

Another heroic figure, this one is adopting a classic pointing stance. His shape is compact and muscled, as a fighter would be. His right leg is standing braced up on a rock incline, which helps to create a dramatic pose. The outfit is a sleeveless leotard with waistband and headband.

Start to detail the head, giving your character large eyes, and a small nose and mouth. His hair is a spiky crop, held by a band. Then flesh out the torso and arms.

Outline the figure using basic shapes: an oval for the head, shoulder, elbow, and knee joints. Add a triangle for the pelvis, then join all the joint lines.

Outline his clothing: a tight-fitting cropped tank top and tight pants with ankle cuffs. Shade these, then shade his headband. Finally, add shaded wristbands.

Next flesh out the legs and feet, which are wide apart. Then add hands. His left hand is pointing, so detail the index finger, and then the other, closed fingers.

NOTHING DOING

A static but powerful pose, this one is useful for situations in which the character needs to stand his ground. The legs are wide apart and ramrod-straight, making a basic A-shape. The arms are folded to present a closed front, and his head is cocked slightly to one side, as if in challenge.

Draw an oval head, add a center vertical line, then bisect it with a line for the shoulders. Add shoulder and knee joints, a triangular pelvis, and lines for arms and legs.

Make a line for the eyes and add them, then sketch his face with a pointed chin. Top this with spiky hair. Add flesh to his folded arms, torso, and legs.

Work on the clothing. He has a tight jacket with a high collar, and tight pants that are baggy around the knee where they fit into boots. Add a crossed belt.

Color his T-shirt black, then color your figure's head pink. Give him red hair. Use gray for his suit. Finally add yellow details on his suit, and color his boots yellow with brown shadows.

Ink your sketch, adding fold lines on the sleeves and pants. Accent the foot of the boots. Then add shadows around the collar, under the folded arms, and on the boots.

41

FALLING CAT-JUMP

This is a dramatic posture, showing a young, athletic fighter falling from above. His arms are raised like a cat, and the shoulders sit high in line with the head to give power to the pose. The legs are split: the right is stretched out ready to land and the left is folded for aerodynamic shape.

Start with an egg shape on its side for the head. Draw one circle above this and one below for the elbow joints, with lines for the arms and a circle for his fist. Add a large oval for his hip. Draw circles for his knee joints and lines for legs and feet.

Create arms and flesh out the torso. Draw his left leg from the hip to the knee joint, then out to the shoe line. Add a shoe. Draw his right leg behind the left. Add his facial features, then give him some spiky hair. Shade this.

He is wearing a loose top with tight cuffs and swinging toggles, loose pants that bunch down his right leg, and martial arts slippers. Draw a sash around his waist, folds and creases in his clothing, and then draw clenched fists.

Ink the main lines, including the creases in his top. Then use black to color his pupils, his hair, and his pants. Leave white highlights down the front of both legs. Color the shadow under his chin and his slippers black, too.

Now use a combination of pink for his skin and dark beige for shadows on his face, hands, and feet. Use a fresh apple-green to color his top and toggles, then use a blue-gray to tone down the highlights on his pants. Finally add a little pale gray to his sash to indicate shadows.

GALLERY

speeding at you

right With a figure that is running like this one, you can enhance the sense of movement by adding speed lines.

subtle

above Coloring can be subtle and still effective. Use cool, dark colors for jackets and trousers, then add some bright touches, such as red for a T-shirt.

unruffled

right This character is calm, confident, and fully aware of the turmoil he is causing to all the young girls around him.

well held

above Add to the dynamism of a leap into the air by adding whoosh lines around the arm.

full of joy

left This character is overjoyed, as evidenced by the huge grin from ear to ear and the jumping figure. The whoosh lines magnify the action.

raging

below Body language can show how a character is feeling. This one is in a rage, with clenched fists and flushed cheeks.

with a pet

left Cute pets are common in manga, and this character is delighted to be playing with his friendly puppy.

LOOKING UPWARD

This face is looking upward at an angle to the top left. You can see the ears are lower with respect to the eyes, and the pupils are raised to the top part of the eye to give a line of vision in that direction. The sharply drawn eyebrows indicate concern and anxiety, while the open mouth suggests she is calling or shouting out.

Draw an oval head, and bisect it horizontally with a curved line nearer the top. Bisect it vertically with a curve nearer to one side than the other. Add the neck.

Sit the pupils on the horizontal line. Add large eyes with double highlights. The visible ear comes from this line, too. Sit the nose and mouth on your vertical line.

Next add the hair. This is short and spiky. Create three pieces for the bangs and front of the hair, and then draw the rest of the hair, starting from the crown.

Outline an area of highlight on each of the bangs. Finally, loosely shade the hair, using a very soft pencil, and shade inside the mouth.

BATTLE CRY

This is a powerful face with mouth open in an aggressive cry, shown by the downturn at the corners of the mouth, and the heavy black eyebrows pointing down to the center. Strong black lines around the eyes increase the intensity of the expression. Her left shoulder is raised and pulled across her face slightly, which suggests she is preparing to deliver a blow.

Start with a pointed oval. Bisect it horizontally and vertically. Create a curve for the front shoulder, a vertical line for the neck, and a curve for the other shoulder.

Draw the large eyes with three areas of highlight, and add arched eyebrows. Add the ears and a small nose. Then draw the large open mouth.

Add the spiky profile of the hair inside the oval. Then give her a long ponytail with a flicked end. Outline a couple of highlights. Then indicate the clothing.

Ink all the main lines, including the folds in the clothes. Then use black to color the hair and the pupils. Finally create the shadow inside the mouth and under the chin.

SMOLDERING FRUSTRATION

Here's another angry expression—this time the face is pointing downward and the eyes are looking angrily up, to give a feeling of barely controlled frustration. The eyes are narrowed and her cheeks are flushed, with the mouth a tiny oval. The sloping hair accentuates the forward tilt of the head.

Start with an egg shape and bisect it horizontally and vertically to help with positioning the features. Add the neck, and bisect this, too.

Add the features, starting with the eyes with double highlights. Add arched eyebrows, then the one visible ear. Add a pert nose and a tiny open mouth.

Give the head some hair next. Work spiky bangs from the top of the oval, and continue it outside the edge of the face. Then add the long locks.

Ink all the main lines, including the areas of detail on the hair. Use a fine pen for the nose and mouth. Then color the pupils black.

Color her face pale pink, using a darker pink for the flush in her cheeks, in her mouth, and under her chin. Give her blue pupils and a mass of yellow hair.

47

ICY GLARE

The face here is that of a cold-hearted person, with an icy stare. The dark, narrow eyes and the thin closed lips mean nothing but trouble. The chin is a sharper point than that of most females, which gives a meaner feel to her face, and the cascading black spikes of her hair are almost spider-like.

Draw a circle, then bisect it vertically. Continue this line down, then sketch two lines to form a V-shape at its base: this will be the chin of the character.

Start to add features, beginning with the eyes and arched eyebrows. Give the figure a small nose and a cupid's bow mouth with a sardonic smile.

Add in the two lines of a hairband across the head, then add the bangs out from this. Then, working from the crown, add the mass of spiky hair.

Ink the main lines of the face, and the upturned collar. Use a fine pen for the nose and mouth. Then use black to color the hair around the areas of highlight.

Now add color. Here the face is pink, with darker shadows on the sides and under her chin. Make her hairband bright green and her top purple. Finally give her red lips.

BABY FACE

Faces can be a good way to show the age of a character. This face is small and wide, so it makes for a younger look. The features are close together in the middle of the face, like a baby's, and she has a petulant expression, with an open, sulky mouth and arched eyebrows.

Draw an oval, with a pointed end. Bisect this with a curved horizontal and a curved vertical: these will help you to position the facial features. Then add a short vertical to indicate a neck.

Start with the eyes, using your curved horizontal as their base. Outline the pupils and give them highlights. Then add arched brows. Use your curved vertical to position the nose and mouth.

Now add hair. Make this a short, spiky style, with chunky bangs and off-center part. Outline a highlight and a clip on the hair. Then add eyelashes.

Ink over the main lines, using a thick nib for the outline, hair, ear, and eye and eyebrow. Use a thinner nib for the nose and mouth. Color the pupils black.

Use shades of beige for the face, with darker shades for the shadow areas under the bangs and chin. Color the pupils honey, then give the figure red hair with a yellow clip.

SAD CONTEMPLATION

This face has a mood of calm but with a sense of unhappiness, indicated by the tightly closed lips and the lightly drawn eyebrows. Her eyes are closed, as shown by the under-arching black lines and the eyelashes, and her hair falls lifelessly down and is a somber white color.

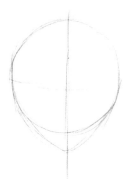

Start by drawing an oval, and bisect this with a vertical line. Draw down to this line to make a chin. Then bisect your circle with a horizontal line.

Use your horizontal line to position the closed eyes and the ears. Add eyebrows, then use your vertical line to position the slightly snubbed nose and thin mouth.

Add the hair next. Use the top of your oval as the line to start your bangs, which are a few thick chunks. Then create the profile of the rest of the hair.

Now ink all the main lines. The eyelashes are one of the dominant features, and the rest of the face and hair is deliberately kept quite simple.

Finally add some color. Use pale pink for the skin, with dark beige for shadow areas in the ears, under the bangs, around the nose and mouth, and under the chin. Then use a cool gray to add shadow to the hair.

DREAMY LONGING

Another closed-eye expression, this one having a wistful, dreamy quality. The head is tilted back and slightly to one side, and the eyebrows are sloping upward. The corners of the mouth are turned up in a hint of a smile. Note the low position of the ear, which emphasizes the angle of the tilt of the head.

Start with an off-center oval as your basic shape. Bisect this horizontally and vertically with curved lines.

Position the main features along your bisecting lines. These include the eyes and the visible ear, together with the nose and mouth. Add eyebrows.

Create spiky bangs with four or five bold points, then add the profile of the rest of the hair, giving it short spiky ends.

Ink over the main lines of the face and hair. At this stage, add highlights in the hair to leave white later.

Color the skin pale pink, with dark pink for the shadow in the mouth, under the bangs, and under the chin. Then, leaving the highlights white, give her blue hair.

51

UNWELCOME SURPRISE

This face has a look of startled alarm on it. The eyes are wide open and slightly downturned. The mouth is also down at the sides, which tells the viewer that the surprise is undoubtedly an unwelcome one. The hairstyle in this case frames the startled eyes nicely, and draws the viewer's attention to the face.

Start with an oval, then work a couple of lines down to a smooth pointed chin. Bisect this oval with curved horizontal and vertical lines.

Add the main features, starting with the eyes. These are wide open, with lots of white around the pupils. Add a tiny snub nose and an open mouth.

Next give the head some hair. Start this higher than the basic oval, and keep the lines smooth and flowing.

Ink the sketch. Outline the face and its features, as well as the hair. Use black to outline the eyes and to color the pupils, which have a highlight.

Finally, color the sketch. Give your figure pale pink skin, with beige shadows under the bangs, along the right-hand jawline, and under the chin. Then give her auburn hair and pale green eyes.

HOPEFUL STARE

Some expressions can be extremely subtle, and these are needed in manga comics where the stories can be complex. The face here is staring head-on at the viewer and shows a hint of hope. The eyes and eyebrows are fairly noncommittal, but the mouth is key. A slight upturn at the corners is hopeful, whereas a slight downturn would change the expression to slight despair.

Draw an oval, then work a vertical line to bisect it. Draw two curving lines down to a pointed chin on the vertical. Finally for this stage, draw a curved horizontal line.

Add the facial features. Position the eyes, with double highlights, and ears on the horizontal line. Work a small nose and mouth on the vertical line.

Then add the hair: keep this fairly simple. Outline a jagged highlight across the top.

Using broad pencil strokes, shade in the hair apart from the top, which is left white. Refine the color in the pupils, then add shading to the neck.

53

HAPPY EXPECTATION

Here is a more positive expression of happiness. The head is turned to a three-quarter angle and is gazing up into the sky. Her eyes are large and healthy-looking, and she has a cute rounded girlish face and features. Her red hair and girlish pigtails emphasize the happy-go-lucky and easygoing expression.

Start by drawing a circle, then bring lines down either side to form a soft chin at the bottom right. Indicate a vertical line for the neck.

Draw another horizontal parallel to, but higher than, the first. Also draw in a curved vertical line to bisect the face.

Add eyes with double highlights across your horizontal line, and draw eyebrows. Use your vertical line as a guide for positioning the nose.

Position an ear across the horizontal line. Then add spiky bangs by drawing in some broad V's. Add some tufts of hair to the left and right of the head.

Next add pigtails, held in place with bobble details. Outline an area of highlight on top of the head.

Use a fine pen to ink over the main lines of the face and hair. Working around the highlights, color the pupils black.

Color your sketch. Use pale pink for the skin, with a darker shade in the ears and on and around the chin. Give the head bright red hair, with green bobbles that secure her pigtails.

LOOKING-DOWN TILT

This head is gently tilted away from the viewer and looking down with a wry smile. Notice the relative positions of the eyes, and how the hair is falling down in a line to follow the tilt. This character's mouth is closed, with a slight upturned smile and a small shadow under the bottom lip to create a slight pout.

Draw a circle, then add a triangle to make a pointed chin. Add a curving line for the neck.

Add a curved horizontal line, then position the eyes on this line. Add eyebrows, then use the bottom of your first circle as the line for the nose.

On the same line as the eyes, add the ear. Then add the mouth underneath the nose.

Draw spikes of hair, working from the crown and across and down to make bangs.

Using a soft pencil and broad strokes, start to shade the eyes and eyebrows. Flesh out the mouth, then shade the spikes of hair, leaving the crown white.

JOYFUL SHOUT

Here's a more animated face, with bright smiling eyes and an open mouth. A hint of the upper teeth helps to give an impression of laughter. This face has soft, youthful curves, which give the character a younger personality.

Start with a circle, then draw a triangle to create a pointed chin.

Bisect your oval both horizontally and vertically to give yourself guides for positioning the features.

Use the horizontal line to position the eyes, with dual highlights, and also the one visible ear. Add a button nose and open mouth.

Give your character spiky cropped hair, working a jagged line across the forehead, and then spikes from the crown.

Ink the main lines, outlining an area of highlight in the hair. Then color the pupils and eyebrows black.

Color the face pale pink, with a darker pink inside the mouth. Then make the area of hair outside the highlight black.

Finally, add shadow inside the ear and under the chin, then color the white highlight in the hair brown.

DISMAY

This boy looks really down in the dumps. The eyebrows, eyes, and mouth are all pointing down, and the eyes are wide open and staring. The mouth has dropped to a low position on the face, and there are double lines underneath the eyes to suggest wrinkles. The hair emphasizes the look by falling straight down in strands.

Start with a circle, then draw a triangle down to make a pointed chin. Add a vertical line here.

Draw the eyes, adding a double highlight in each. Then add eyebrows. Add ears to the same line as the eyes.

Add a tiny nose, then add an open mouth. Refine the ears.

Create a spiky hairstyle by working bangs, then start from the crown and work to left and right. Outline a highlight across the top of the hair.

Ink all the important lines, then use black to color the pupils, except the highlights, and the hair, again leaving the highlight white.

PROFILE WITH FOCUS

Here's an example of how positioning and angle can give meaning to a face. Although this is a normal profile view, the forward angle of the neck and narrowed eyes lend an air of intent to this red-headed male character. The nose exaggerates this by being a sharper point than usual, and the loose hair dropping vertically frames it nicely.

  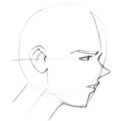 

Start with a circle, then draw two lines to come to a point for the chin.

Create the profile by making an indentation for the eye, and adding a snub nose and slightly open mouth.

Add the eye and eyebrow, based on your horizontal line. Use this line as the midline for the ear.

Now add hair. Start from the crown and work in both directions. Outline an area of highlight on the top.

Ink the outline of the face and hair. Ink the eye and the eyebrow, as well as the ear.

Introduce some color, using a flat pink for the face and bright orange for the hair.

Finally, add more detail to the color. Create shade under the chin and under the bangs. There is also an area of shadow in the ear.

EXASPERATION

You can make your character more masculine by having a wider, squared-off jaw and a broad neck. This face could belong to a muscle-bound hero or villain. His head is topped by a hard-looking hairstyle, and his eyes are ringed by heavy black linework and severe eyebrows. The pupils are small black circles, which give a cold touch to the face.

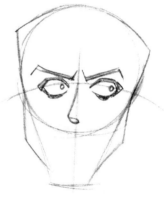

Start by drawing a circle for the head, then draw two lines down, and one horizontal line to square off the chin.

Define the shape of the head a little more, squaring off the top and the jawline.

Draw a vertical center line and a curved horizontal line to help position the features. Add the large eyes with small pupils, knitted eyebrows, and the nose.

Add the ears, positioning them on your horizontal line. Then add the mouth.

Around the existing profile, add in the hairline. Then using broad strokes with a soft pencil, shade this in. As a finishing touch, refine the shape of the mouth.

CONFIDENT SMILE

This character has an intelligent, knowing smile on his face. The head is tilted slightly down, so he has to look through his fringe, which makes him look slightly sinister. The eyes are almond-shaped with dark lashes, and he has long, slender, arched eyebrows. His mouth has the smallest of dimples on one side, which can be used to denote a smirk.

Start by drawing a circle, then add two lines to create the profile of the chin.

Add curved horizontal and vertical lines to help with positioning the facial features.

Outline the eyes, then add in eyebrows.

Get some detail into the eyes by working the pupils, leaving a double highlight in each one. Then add the nose.

Next add some hair. Make this a short, spiky style, and indicate a highlight across the top of the head.

Ink all the main lines, making sure that the bangs sit on top of the eyebrows. Color the pupils black, except for the double highlights.

Make his face pale pink, with browner shadows beneath the bangs, in the ear, and below the chin. Then, working around the highlight, color the hair black.

ALARM CALL

Looking up and across in alarm, this face is dramatic and engaging. The upturned angle gives the character a vulnerable look, and the small lines on each cheek suggest a flush of anxiety. Small pupils in the center of the whites of the eyes accentuate the look of fear on his face.

Draw an oval to start the basic head, then add two lines to make a point for the chin.

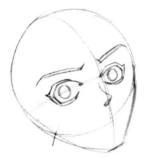

Create a horizontal and a vertical center line, then outline eyes on the horizontal. Add eyebrows and a nose.

Add an ear, using the horizontal line as a guide to positioning. Then add an open mouth.

Now add a mass of spiky hair. Work from the ear across the forehead to create bangs, then add spikes on top of the head. Draw in the pupils.

Ink your sketch. Break the lines of the eyebrows so that the bangs sit on top of them. Add shading details to the cheeks and inside the mouth.

GOOFY GRIN

This is a difficult but very effective expression. A grin can indicate embarrassment when coupled with heavy-lidded eyes and flushed cheeks. Note how the teeth are shown clenched in a forced and unnatural manner, and the eyebrows are rising in a hopeful way.

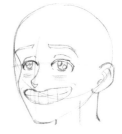

Draw a circle to start with, then add two lines to make a point for the chin.

Bisect the head with a vertical line and a horizontal line to help you to position the features.

Start with the eyes, adding pupils with double highlights. Then add eyebrows.

Now draw the nose and mouth. The mouth here is large and open, and, unusually, has clearly defined teeth.

From a center line draw two uprights, then create two areas of spiky bangs. Add hair to the top and back of the head.

Ink all the important lines of the sketch and color the pupils black. Then use black to create the darkest area of hair.

Use pale pink for the face, then add shadow with a dark beige under the bangs, in the ear, and under the chin. Leaving white highlights, color the hair blue.

GRIEF AND MISERY

Some days are better than others, and this shows one of the bad ones. This face is creased and crumpled with crying. The tears streaming from his tightly closed eyes, and the grimace on his mouth show this character is suffering. Tears can be drawn rolling down the cheeks to the chin for maximum effect.

Draw a circle, then add two lines coming to a point to create the shape of the chin.

To help with positioning the features, bisect your head with a vertical and a horizontal line.

Start with the eyes, even though these are squeezed shut. Draw them as curled lines, then add the eyebrows.

Next add the nose and mouth. The mouth is open and the teeth are visible, although undefined.

Then add the visible ear, and use this to help you to add spiky cropped hair.

Create the tears coming from his eyes. Finally, leaving areas of white highlight, lightly shade your character's hair.

REALIZATION DAWNS

This character has just realized his mistake and feels a definite sense of chagrin about it. His deadpan expression and dilated pupils make him look stunned, and the position of his mouth, represented by a narrow downward-curving line, enforces his dismay.

Begin by drawing a circle, then add a U-shape to create the line of the chin.

Create a horizontal line for the eyeline, then add large, open eyes with a small circular pupil.

Use the same horizontal line to guide you in placing the ears. Then add a small nose and small, thin, down-turned mouth.

Add a headband, then work spiky bangs from this right across the forehead.

Add more spiky hair on top of the head, taking this over the line of the headband, too.

Ink all the lines, making sure you establish where the hair sits on top of the band.

Introduce some color. Use pale pink for the face, with beige shadows. Make the band blue, and color the hair in tones of brown and green.

EXPRESSIONS

A good way to practice expressions is to use the same head, and vary the eyes and mouth to create different looks, as has been done here and opposite. You can also see from these expressions how shading can be used in different positions to vary the facial expression. Draw a series of outline heads and hair, and practice.

This is a dejected expression: the dropped eyebrows and down-sloping eyes, sidelong glance, and worry lines all point to dejection.

A determined expression is characterized by drawn-down eyebrows and flat, hooded tops to the eyes.

An open, laughing mouth and closed eyes with raised eyebrows show that this character is in a happy mood.

This character has a horrified expression. The eyes are huge, but the pupils are tiny dots. The mouth is twisted in a terrified yell.

With eyebrows and eyes sloping upward, this character is smitten. The pupils have been replaced by hearts to add to the effect.

The perfect oval of the mouth, the wide-open eyes, and the raised eyebrows show that this character has been surprised.

EMOTIONS

You will only get emotion into your characters by practicing. Look at the examples here and pinpoint the major features that characterize each emotion. The eyes are always important and the mouth can be a critical feature. The same basic face here is used to convey six totally different emotions from overjoyed to furious.

This girl is furious. The shape of the eyes, and the arched eyebrows, and the tight, down-curving mouth are ample demonstration of her fury.

Surprise can be indicated by the round, staring eyes and small pupils. The shading lines under the eyes denote a slight anxiety or nervousness.

The large, smiling mouth and closed eyes with downward curves suggest this girl is extremely happy. The shading on the nose makes it look cute.

This girl is alluring: her dark, smoldering eyes with large pupils, and her feminine lips point to her being a seductress.

Chagrin is a difficult emotion to convey. Here the closed eyes on an upward curve denote shameful embarrassment.

Happy, calm, and placid is a useful emotion for many characters. This wide-eyed girl has an innocent expression.

GALLERY

furious
below Red hair always points to a fiery temperament and a hint of danger. This character is in a fight, with his wide-open mouth suggesting a yell of defiance.

frustrated
above Dramatic spikes in subdued colors suggest frustration, a look complemented by this boy's drawn brow, grimacing mouth, and strong shadows on the face and hair.

dejected
above The dark hair here complements the dark eyes, with rings under them. His skin tone is washed out, too: this character clearly has had a bad day.

innocent
left Wide eyes with close pupils and a shock of blue hair point to an innocent, happy character.

drenched

right The weather can do great things to hair. Here the rain has plastered it in streaks to the character's face.

sinister

below A shock of crown hair lit from below, together with the large eyes, point to a rather sinister character.

handsome youth

right This is a great look for a bishounen male: these characters are always slightly androgynous with fashionable hair and clothes.

far out

right Dramatic characters need dramatic coloring. Here the dark skin and brooding eyes are complemented by the shock of white hair.

rebellious

below Wide eyes and mouth, together with a cropped, spiky hairstyle, position this young, lively character as something of a rebel.

rock chick

right This character has a cute face with wide, innocent eyes, and a rock'n'roll hairstyle that has a touch of glamour, too.

strong

right Flowing locks colored dark green and gray add an air of strength to this character. She could be a fighter in a traditional manga action story.

punk

above Spiky hair contributes to a punk look, and this boy's wide-open eyes and sneering mouth add to the defiant impression.

free spirit

above Bright blue is a good hair color for a punky hairstyle. This wide-eyed character is feisty and free-spirited.

pensive

above The head on one side shows a thoughtful nature, a look emphasized by his eyes, staring in the same direction as his head is cocked.

youthful

above Large, innocent blue eyes and plaits of pigtails tend to say a character is young and vulnerable. The blonde hair adds to this effect.

tender

left This character's look is fairly neutral: he may be paying attention or he may not. His face shows a sympathetic expression.

GLOSSARY

bisect To cut in two; to divide into two equal parts.

bleed v. To ooze, run together, or spread beyond its proper boundary (as in ink); n. the part of a printed picture or design that overruns the margin.

coy Bashful; a shrinking from contact or familiarity with others; primly reserved; pretending to be innocent or shy.

demure Modest; reserved.

ellipse A closed curve.

emotive Characterized by, expressing, or producing emotion; relating to the emotions.

epaulette A shoulder ornament for certain uniforms (usually military uniforms) or on women's dresses.

foreshorten To represent some lines of an object or figure as shorter than they actually are in order to give the illusion of proper relative size according to principles of visual perspective.

freehand Drawn or done by hand without the use of instruments or measurements.

gouache A pigment made of opaque colors ground in water and mixed with a preparation of gum.

graphic novel A narrative work in which the story is conveyed to the reader using sequential art in either an experimental design or a traditional comics format.

The term can apply to nonfiction works, thematically linked short stories, serial fiction, and long-form fiction.

inking Placing refined outlines over pencil lines using black ink and a pen, brush, or computer.

kimono A loose outer garment with short, wide sleeves and a sash; a traditional garment of Japanese men and women.

layout The manner in which something is arranged and/or illustrated, such as an advertisement, newspaper, book, or page.

majorette A person who leads a marching band or precedes it while twirling a baton.

manga Comics and print cartoons usually written in Japanese, published in Japan, and partaking of a Japanese style of illustration first developed in the late nineteenth century. Manga-inspired comics and graphic novels are now produced worldwide, but "manga" still generally refers to comics of Japanese origin.

medium The singular of "media"; any material or technique used for the creation of art; a means of communication to the general public.

opaque Not letting light pass through; not transparent or translucent; not reflecting light; not shining or lustrous; dull or dark.

perspective The art of picturing objects or a scene in such a way as to show them as they appear to the eye with relative distance or depth; the appearance of objects or scenes as determined by their relative distance and positions.

pigment A coloring matter, usually in the form of an insoluble powder mixed with oil or water to make paints.

static Not moving or progressing; at rest; inactive; stationary.

FOR MORE INFORMATION

Comic-Con International
P.O. Box 128458
San Diego, CA 92112-8458
(619) 491-2475
Web site: http://www.comic-con.org
Comic-Con International is a nonprofit educational organiza-
    tion dedicated to creating awareness of, and appreciation
    for, comics and related popular art forms, primarily
    through the presentation of conventions and events that
    celebrate the historic and ongoing contribution of comics
    to art and culture.

Dark Horse Comics
10956 SE Main Street
Milwaukie, OR 97222
(503) 652-8815
Web site: http://www.darkhorse.com
Founded in 1986 by Mike Richardson, Dark Horse Comics
    has grown to become the third-largest comics publisher
    in the United States and is acclaimed internationally
    for the quality and diversity of its line and its ability to
    attract the top talent in the comics field. In conjunction
    with its sister company, Dark Horse Entertainment, Dark
    Horse has over 350 properties currently represented

under the Dark Horse banner, serving as the jumping-off
point for comics, books, films, television, electronic
games, toys, and collectibles. Dark Horse distributes its
characters and concepts into more than fifty countries.

Del Rey Graphic Novels and Manga
Random House Publishing
1745 Broadway
New York, NY 10019
(212) 782-9000
Web site: http://graphic-novels-manga.suvudu.com
Del Rey Manga is a division of U.S. publisher Random
House, working in conjunction with Kodansha, a leading
Japanese manga publisher. With a primary focus on
shojo and shonen manga titles, Del Rey Manga has
established itself as the fourth-largest publisher of
Japanese comics in English.

Fantagraphics Books
7563 Lake City Way NE
Seattle, WA 98115
(206) 524-1967
Web site: http://www.fantagraphics.com
Fantagraphics Books has been a leading proponent of comics as a legitimate form of art and literature since it began
publishing the critical trade magazine the Comics Journal
in 1976. By the early 1980s, Fantagraphics was at the
forefront of the successful movement to establish comics
as a medium as expressive and worthy as the more
established popular arts of film, literature, and poetry.
Fantagraphics has since gained an international reputation

for its literate and innovative editorial standards and its superb production values. Fantagraphics was ranked among the top five most influential publishers in the history of comics in a recent poll by an industry trade newspaper.

Kodansha International
Otowa YK Building 1-17-14
Otowa, Bunkyo-ku, Tokyo
Japan 112-8652
Tel.: 81-3-3944-6491
Web site: http://www.kodansha-intl.com
Kodansha is Japan's largest publisher. Originally established in 1909 by Seiji Noma, the company is still a family-run business. Kodansha continues to play a dominant role in the media world, producing books and magazines in a wide variety of genres including literature, fiction, nonfiction, children's, business, lifestyle, art, manga, fashion, and journalism. Recently, the company has ventured into digital distribution of content as well.

TOKYOPOP
Variety Building
5900 Wilshire Boulevard, 20th Floor
Los Angeles, CA 90036-5020
(323) 692-6700
Web site: http://www.tokyopop.com/manga
Founded in 1997 by media entrepreneur Stu Levy, TOKYOPOP established the market for manga in North America, introducing the term to the English language in the process. TOKYOPOP has published over three

thousand books, distributed anime and Asian films on home video and television, licensed merchandise to consumer goods companies, and created graphic novels of major brands such as Warcraft, Star Trek, SpongeBob SquarePants, and Hannah Montana. TOKYOPOP expanded internationally with offices in Europe and Japan and a network of over 160 partners in more than 50 countries and 30 languages.

VIZ Media, LLC
P.O. BOX 77010
San Francisco, CA 94107
Web site: http://www.viz.com
One of the first companies to publish Japanese manga for the U.S. market, VIZ Media publishes and distributes comics, graphic novels, novel adaptations of manga, magazines, art books, and children's books. VIZ also releases anime DVDs and handles licensing for its manga and animation properties.

WEB SITES
Due to the changing nature of Internet links, Rosen Publishing has developed an online list of Web sites related to the subject of this book. This site is updated regularly. Please use this link to access the list:

http://www.rosenlinks.com/mm/pose

Amberlyn, J. C. *Drawing Manga Animals, Chibis, and Other Adorable Creatures.* New York, NY: Watson-Guptill, 2009.

Comickers Magazine. *Comickers Art: Tools and Techniques for Drawing Amazing Manga.* New York, NY: Harper Design, 2008.

Comickers Magazine. *Comickers Art 2: Create Amazing Manga Characters.* New York, NY: Collins Design, 2008.

Comickers Magazine. *Comickers Art 3: Write Amazing Manga Stories.* New York, NY: Harper Design, 2008.

Flores, Irene. *Shojo Fashion Manga Art School: How to Draw Cool Looks and Characters.* Cincinnati, OH: IMPACT Books, 2009.

Hart, Christopher. *Manga for the Beginner: Everything You Need to Start Drawing Right Away!* New York, NY: Watson-Guptill, 2008.

Hart, Christopher. *Manga for the Beginner Chibis: Everything You Need to Start Drawing the Super-Cute Characters of Japanese Comics.* New York, NY: Watson-Guptill, 2010.

Hart, Christopher. *Manga for the Beginner Shoujo:*

Everything You Need to Start Drawing the Most Popular Style of Japanese Comics. New York, NY: Watson-Guptill, 2010.

Hart, Christopher. *Manga Mania: Chibi and Furry Characters: How to Draw the Adorable Mini-Characters and Cool Cat-Girls of Japanese Comics.* New York, NY: Watson-Guptill, 2006.

Hills, Doug. *Manga Studio for Dummies.* Hoboken, NJ: Wiley Publishing, Inc., 2008.

Joso, Estudio, ed. *The Monster Book of Manga: Draw Like the Experts.* New York, NY: Harper Design, 2006.

Ikari Studio, ed. *The Monster Book of Manga: Boys.* New York, NY: Harper Design, 2010.

Ikari Studio, ed. *The Monster Book of Manga: Fairies and Magical Creatures: Draw Like the Experts.* New York, NY: Harper Design, 2007.

Ikari Studio, ed. *The Monster Book of Manga: Girls.* New York, NY: Harper Design, 2008.

Okabayashi, Kensuke. *Manga for Dummies.* Hoboken, NJ: Wiley Publishing, Inc., 2007.

Takarai, Saori. *Manga Moods: 40 Faces and 80 Phrases.* Saitama, Japan: Japanime Co., Ltd., 2006.

Thompson, Jason. *Manga: The Complete Guide.* New York, NY: Del Ray, 2007.

INDEX

ABOUT THE AUTHORS

Anna Southgate is an experienced writer and editor who has worked extensively for publishers of adult illustrated reference books. Her recent work has included art instruction books and providing the text for a series of six manga titles.

Keith Sparrow has read and collected comics since he was a child. He has created hundreds of storyboards, including one for the animation movie *Space Jam*, and illustrated several children's educational books for the UK's Channel 4 and the BBC. He became a fan of manga and anime after reading Akira.